All Around America

The Study Guide
for
The Time Traveler's Talk Show

J D Rivera
Talk Show Host

Raymond C. Clark
Anne Siebert

PRO LINGUA ASSOCIATES

Pro Lingua Associates, Publishers
P.O. Box 1348
Brattleboro, Vermont 05302 USA
Office: 802 257 7779
Orders: 800 366 4775
E-mail: info@ProLinguaAssociates.com
WebStore www.ProLinguaAssociates.com
SAN: 216-0579

*At Pro Lingua
our objective is to foster an approach
to learning and teaching that we call
interplay, the **inter**action of language
learners and teachers with their materials,
with the language and culture,
and with each other in active, creative
and productive **play**.*

Copyright © 2004 by Raymond C. Clark and Anne Siebert

ISBN 0-86647-184-7

This book was designed by Arthur A. Burrows. The text was set in Bookman Oldstyle, a modern, bold adaptation of a traditional square serif face; it is an Agfa digital font. The cover display type is Trebuchet. The book was printed and bound by Capital City Press in Montpelier, Vermont.

Illustrations in this book have come from the following sources: Art Explosion 750,000 Images™ (© 2000 Nova Development Corporation); The Big Box of Art™ (© 2001 Hermera Technologies, Inc.™); p. 34 by Missy Beaver, Oregon Trail South Central Co-op; and personal photos.

Printed in the United States of America
First printing 2004. 1000 copies.

Contents

Introduction

All Around America: The Time Traveler's Talk Show with its companion ***Study Guide*** is an intermediate-advanced level program for English language learners. The talk show text is a dramatic reader which the learners use as a cooperative reading experience. The eighteen units (shows) explore the history, culture, and nature of the United States and provide opportunities to develop English language skills.

This Study Guide maximizes the development of language skills by providing a variety of exercises that will enable the learners to get the most out of their learning experience.

The text and the study guide can be used in a variety of ways. **The *recommended procedure* is as follows:**

1. **Begin with the Study Guide**. Introduce the locale and engage the students in an initial discussion:

   Where is the Statue of Liberty?
   What does it look like?
   Has anybody seen it?

2. **Do Part A**. This prepares the learners for the nouns that are crucial for understanding the content of the talk show. One procedure would be to have the students look at the list of nouns in Part A and check off the ones they think they know. Then as a class or in pairs they try to establish meaning for the unknowns. Or, they can proceed to:

3. **Part B.** The nouns in the list in Part A are highlighted in the reading. By reading Part B, the learners can begin to sense the meanings of the nouns by seeing them in the context of phrases and sentences. At the same time, the reading prepares the students for what they will read and hear in the talk show script.

4. **Part C.** This exercise is basically a matching exercise that prepares the learners for the idioms and expressions they will encounter in the talk show. Although this can be done by individuals, pairs will have to use English together to make the matches. In most cases, the matches are obvious, but answers are provided in the back of the Study Guide.

5. **Do the talk show**. (See the introduction to the talk show for details.)

   A. Assign parts and have the learners read their lines aloud.

   B. Read through the script again.

   C. Use the Fact Sheets.

   D. Do a final, dramatic reading, record it, and play it back.

6. **Return to the Study Guide and do the True-False Review.** This simple activity reviews the show and checks comprehension. The learners should do this without looking back at the talk show script. The answers are in the back. After checking their answers, the learners can look back at the script. Mistakes often lead to learning. The learners can be encouraged to keep a record of their comprehension scores. As they work through the talk show, their scores should show improvement and progress.

7. **Exercise E. Vocabulary Review.** This exercise is more of a challenge than the true-false exercise. The learners have to recall and write a few selected words. This is probably best done by individuals.

8. **Exercise F.** This is a summary of the adjectives used in the show. It can be used in a variety of ways. One way is to call out an adjective and have the learners respond with a noun that collocates with the adjective. The learners can also look back through the talk show to find the adjective and how it is used. The order of the adjectives in the list follows the order in which they appear in the talk show. As the learners continue through the shows, they will notice that there is recycling of the adjectives.

9. **Exercise G.** This is an opportunity to practice writing on a topic that relates to the show. This can be a homework assignment.

10. **Assign Exercise H**. Encourage the learners to go to the web and explore the topic in greater detail. They can report on their virtual visit the next time the class meets.

The Statue of Liberty

A Beacon of Freedom

A. PREVIEW. Do you know these words? Look for them in the reading below.

____ statue	____ sculptor	____ contribution	____ beacon
____ liberty	____ framework	____ crown	____ monument
____ symbol	____ pedestal	____ harbor	____ treasure
____ freedom	____ achievement	____ torch	

B. Read this selection.

The **Statue** of **Liberty** is one of America's great **symbols**. It stands for **freedom**.

Frederic Bartholdi was the **sculptor** of the statue. It was a birthday gift for America from France. It is a gorgeous and colossal statue. It took over ten years to construct the statue. Alexander Eiffel designed the internal **framework** of the statue. He also created the Eiffel Tower in Paris.

The statue needed a pedestal. Joseph Pulitzer was an immigrant who became the owner of a newspaper — The New York World. The idea of freedom and the statue was important to him. With his newspaper he helped raise money for the platform that Liberty would stand on. People all across America gave money to build the **pedestal** for the statue. Money came from everywhere. The response was wonderful. It was inspiring.

Like many immigrants, Pulitzer made many important **contributions** to this country. He also established a prize for outstanding **achievement** in letters.

Many immigrants and refugees saw this great statue when they sailed into New York harbor. Some of them were escaping from terrible situations in other countries. They were processed and admitted on nearby Ellis Island. The island is now a museum.

Visitors to the statue can go all the way up to the **crown**. From there the view of New York is a wonderful sight. And from the city and the **harbor** you can see the **torch** shining at night. It is a **beacon** showing people the way to freedom. This wonderful **monument** is a national **treasure**.

Exercises

C. Do you know these idioms and expressions? Work with a partner and put them in the sentences below.

stands for	ran out of	one and the same
near and dear	knock __ down	in person
on the line	take __ for granted	Absolutely
In the first place	By the way	tune in
coming up		

1. The phone is ringing. Hello, Mr. Pulitzer, are you ____ _____ _____?

2. Americans sometimes _____ freedom _____ _____ They don't appreciate it and realize how important it is.

3. A: So, Mr. Pulitzer, you were the owner of the New York World. ____ _____ _____ sir, are you the same man who established the Pulitzer Prize?

   B: Yes, J D. That's me, _____ _____ _____ _____

4. Don't forget to _____ ____ to our program next week when we are in Boston.

5. Why did you do that? Well, there were a few reasons. ____ _____ _____ _____, I wanted to give America a birthday gift.

6. Lady Liberty _____ _____ freedom. She's a symbol.

7. It was important that winds would not _____ the statue _____ and destroy it.

8. America's birthday was _____ ____. It would be very soon.

9. Freedom is an idea that is _____ _____ _____ to many Americans. It's very important to them.

10. I've seen pictures of the statue, but I've never seen it ____ _____.

11. Can you really go inside the statue? _____! You can go all the way up to her crown.

12. They _____ _____ ____ money several times and had to stop working.

4   **The Statue of Liberty**

Exercises

D. What do you remember? After you do the talk show, answer this true or false review.

1. _____ Frederic Bartholdi was an engineer.

2. _____ The statue was a gift from France.

3. _____ There was not enough money to pay for the crown.

4. _____ Joseph Pulitzer was a famous artist.

5. _____ Pulitzer was an immigrant from France.

6. _____ Americans contributed thousands of dollars for the pedestal.

7. _____ Construction was stopped because they ran out of money.

8. _____ The torch shines all night.

9. _____ The Pulitzer Prize is given for achievement in science.

10. _____ Bartholdi also created the Eiffel Tower.

Number right _____/10

E. Vocabulary Review. Finish these sentences.

1. A light shining in the distance is a _____.

2. The inside structure of something is called the _____.

3. A statue stands on a _____.

4. The Statue of Liberty holds a _____ in her hand.

Exercises

5. On her head is a _____

6. The statue _____ _____ freedom.

7. A _____ creates statues.

8. The statue is very big. It is _____

9. The statue can be seen from a ship in the New York _____

10. It took over ten years to _____ the statue.

Number right _____/10

F. These adjectives are used in the talk show. Can you use them?

For example: great > a great sculptor   beautiful > The statue is beautiful.

timeless _____   beautiful _____
important _____   wonderful _____
famous _____   special _____
proud _____   terrible _____
mobile _____   huge _____
inspiring _____   thankful _____
great _____   internal _____
outstanding _____   homeless _____

G. On a separate piece of paper, write a letter to a friend about your first day in a new country. Write about when and why you came and how you felt on that day.

H. Check out these websites on the internet. Tell or write about something that you found interesting.

www.nps.gov/stli/   (Statue of Liberty National Monument)

www. nyctourist.com/liberty/.htm   (A photo tour)

www.nps.gov/elis/   (Ellis Island)

The Statue of Liberty

Boston

A Walk in Revolutionary America

A. PREVIEW. Do you know these words? Look for them in the reading below.

____ trail	____ advocate	____ lantern	____ attack
____ revolution	____ taxation	____ steeple	____ retreat
____ massacre	____ representation	____ militia	____ casualty
____ mob	____ parliament	____ battle	

B. Read this selection.

The Freedom **Trail** is a 2.5 mile walking tour in Boston, Massachusetts. The American **Revolution** began in the Boston area. There are many historic highlights along the trail, and one of them is the site of the Boston **Massacre**. At this spot, a group of Colonials, angry about the taxes imposed on them by the British government, gathered and confronted some British soldiers. The soldiers panicked and fired on the **mob**, killing five people. One was a former slave, Crispus Attucks, an African American.

A Boston lawyer, John Adams, defended the soldiers in court and won. Adams was also a patriot, an **advocate** of the rights of the colonists, and he became a leader of the Revolution and later the second president of the United States.

Another patriot, Samuel Adams, organized a protest called the Boston Tea Party. The protesters were still angry about the British taxes. They believed that **taxation** without **representation** was not fair. They should have representatives in the British **parliament**. They boarded some British ships in the harbor and threw boxes of tea off the ships to protest the tax.

Another stop on the Freedom Trail is the Old North Church where a patriot put a **lantern** in the church **steeple** to warn that the British were going to march to nearby Concord to capture colonial leaders and disarm the **militia**. Three men, including Paul Revere, rode to Concord to warn the militia. In Lexington and Concord the colonials fired at the British, killing several.

The **Battle** of Bunker Hill was the first major battle of the Revolution. The colonial army occcupied a hill and defended it against three **attacks** by the British. The colonials finally **retreated** and the British took the hill, but they had many **casualties**, dead and wounded.

Exercises

C. Do you know these idioms and expressions? Work with a partner and put them in the sentences below.

out of the question	stand by	on the way
filled in	jump in	got away
better half	sick and tired	stood their ground
all over again	hot on their trail	underway
ran away	fans the flames	

1. This has got to stop! We're _____ _____ _____ of these heavy taxes. Enough is enough!

2. Stay there! Help is _____ _____ _____ and should be there soon.

3. Every time Adams gives a speech, he only _____ _____ _____. The situation is becoming dangerous.

4. No! No way! That's _____ _____ _____ _____.

5. They escaped, but the army was _____ _____ _____ _____ and almost caught them.

6. The president was very busy, but the vice-president _____ _____ for him and gave a speech.

7. This is my _____ _____. I've been married to her for 20 years.

8. They caught two of them, but one _____ _____ and arrived safely in Concord.

9. I didn't want to do it, but I had to. I don't regret it, and I would do it _____ _____ _____.

10. We may need your help. Can you _____ _____ and _____ _____ if necessary?

11. The young army didn't retreat. They _____ _____ _____ and fought bravely. And that was the beginning. The Revolution was _____.

12. After he _____ _____ from home, he went to sea for several years.

Exercises

D. What do you remember? After you do the talk show, do this true or false review.

1. _____ The Freedom Trail is over ten miles long.

2. _____ Only five people were killed in the Boston Massacre.

3. _____ Abigail Adams was John Adams' sister.

4. _____ John Adams became President of the United States.

5. _____ Paul Revere organized the Boston Tea Party.

6. _____ Indians threw tea into the Boston Harbor.

7. _____ The British tried to catch Sam Adams and George Washington in Concord.

8. _____ The Old North Church is on the Freedom Trail.

9. _____ The Colonial Militia fired at the British in Lexington and Concord.

10. _____ The Battle of Bunker Hill was fought near Boston.

Number right _____ / 10

E. Vocabulary Review. Finish these sentences.

1. Abigail Adams was the _____ of John Adams.

2. The British soldiers were called _____.

3. John Adams _____ the British soldiers in court.

4. The colonists were tired of paying _____ on tea.

5. The British were planning to _____ to Concord.

6. Paul Revere saw a _____ in the steeple of the Old North Church.

7. The British planned to _____ some hills near Boston.

Exercises

8. The British _____ three times.

9. The Colonial Army finally _____.

10. There were many _____ on both sides, many dead and wounded.

Number right _____/10

Paul Revere's House on the Boston Freedom Trail

F. These adjectives are used in the talk show. Can you use them with a noun or the verb *to be*?

For example: big > We went to a <u>big city</u>. **or:** This city <u>is big.</u>

____ appropriate	____ angry	____ ready	____ final
____ early	____ popular	____ underway	____ victorious
____ upset	____ strong	____ major	____ brave
____ heavy	____ ironic	____ defensive	____ bloody

G. On a separate piece of paper, write about one of these topics:

a. A revolution in another country.
b. An unfair tax.
c. A famous battle.

H. Check out one of these websites on the internet. Tell or write about something you found interesting.

www.thefreedomtrail.org
www.nps.gov/bost/freedom_trail.htm

Exercises

Lowell

The Industrial Revolution in America

A. PREVIEW. Do you know these words? Look for them in the reading below.

____ flow	____ textiles	____ environment	____ labor
____ turbine	____ showplace	____ boarding house	____ festival
____ machinery	____ industry	____ wages	____ diversity
____ mill	____ model	____ immigrant	

B. Read this selection.

The Lowell National Historical Park is significant because it is the birthplace of the American Industrial Revolution. In Lowell, the Merrimack River **flows** rapidly, and as a result, a lot of water power is available to turn the water wheels and **turbines** which operate the **machinery**. And so, **mills** were built all along the river.

The principal product was **textiles**, and the city became the **showplace** of American **industry**. Many famous people visited Lowell because it was an outstanding **model** of an industrial city. The writer Henry David Thoreau was very impressed with industrialization. However, he also saw that there were **environmental** problems.

The mills needed labor, and they attracted young women from New England towns and farms. They lived in **boardinghouses** and had many opportunities, but they worked long hours and demanded higher **wages**.

By the middle of the 19th century, **immigrants** began to pour into Lowell. They were willing to work long hours for little money. The mill owners were happy to have cheap **labor**. As a result, Lowell became a city of many ethnic neighborhoods.

Many French Canadians lived in Lowell. One of them was Jack Kerouac. He was an important American writer of the 20th century. Every year Lowell has a **festival** to honor him.

In the 20th century, Lowell suffered economic disaster. The mills closed and moved south. Lowell began to die, but eventually it came back to life with new industries. Nowadays, Lowell is still a city of great cultural and ethnic **diversity**.

Exercises

C. Do you know these idioms and expressions? Work with a partner and put them in the sentences below.

put out   On the one hand   keep up
a great deal of   in my mind   grew up
named after   shut down   laid off
pick up   take advantage of   dropped out
                       wrap up

1. My brother is _____ _____ my grandfather. They have the same name.

2. The turbines could produce ___ _____ _____ ____ power.

3. ____ _____ _____ _____ the pay wasn't bad, but on the other, the hours were long.

4. The mills _____ _____ millions of yards of cloth every year.

5. Because of competition, many companies couldn't _____ ____. They had to _____ _____ or move south.

6. Cities in the South were competitive because they could _____ _____ ____ a warmer climate.

7. I'll _____ ____ the story from here, and at the end, you can _____ it ____.

8. Basically, I agree with you, but ____ ____ _____ I think the mill owners didn't really understand the situation.

9. She _____ ____ on a small farm and moved to the city when she was only 18.

10. It was difficult to study and work, so he _____ _____ of school.

11. When the mill closed he got _____ _____ and had to look for work.

Exercises

D. What do you remember? After you do the talk show, do this true or false review.

1. _____ Francis Cabot Lowell built his first mill on the Merrimack River.

2. _____ The mills of Lowell produced cloth.

3. _____The mills used water to produce power.

4. _____ Francis Cabot Lowell visited Manchester, New Hampshire to study the textile industry.

5. _____ Henry David Thoreau was a mill owner.

6. _____ By the middle of the 1950s, most mills were shut down.

7. _____ The mill girls came from Ireland.

8. _____ The mill girls worked 12 hours a day.

9. _____ The writer Jack Kerouac grew up speaking French.

10. _____ Kerouac graduated from Columbia University.

Number right _____/10

The Mills of Lowell

E. Vocabulary Review. Finish these sentences.

1. Lowell was the _____ of the American Industrial Revolution.

2. The mills in Lowell produced _____.

3. The Merrimack River _____ very rapidly in Lowell.

4. The flowing water turned the water wheels and the _____.

5. Many people came to see Lowell because it was the _____ of the American Industrial Revolution.

6. In the 19th century, _____ began to _____ into the country.

7. The mill girls lived in _____.

8. The Kerouac family was originally from _____.

9. In 1957 Kerouac's novel became a _____.

10. Lowell is a multi-_____ city.

Number right _____/10

F. These adjectives are used in the talk show. Can you use them ?

____ significant	____ surprised	____ rich	____ ethnic
____ main	____ abundant	____ clean	____ difficult
____ impressed	____ young	____ cheap	____ alive
____ successful	____ single		

G. On a separate piece of paper, write about one of these topics:

a. An industry in our town/city.
b. My experience as an immigrant.
c. My job.

H. Check out one of these websites on the internet. Take notes and report on your visit.

www.nps.gov/lowe (National Historical Park)

www.ci.lowell.ma.us/ (City of Lowell)

www.cmgww.com/historic/kerouac/ (Jack Kerouac)

Gettysburg
Civil War Battlefield

A. PREVIEW. Do you know these words? Look for them in the reading below.

____ civil war   ____ issue   ____ victory   ____ rifles
____ Union   ____ economy   ____ defeat   ____ cemetery
____ Confederacy   ____ army   ____ re-enactments   ____ address
____ conflict   ____ loss   ____ buffs   ____ memorial
____ slavery   ____ general   ____ uniform

B. Read this selection.

Gettysburg National Military Park is in the hills of Pennsylvania. It is the site of an important battle in America's **Civil War.** It was a bloody battle between the northern states, called the **Union**, and the southern states, called the **Confederacy**.

The South wanted to be an independent country and so they seceded from the United States. There were many causes for this tragic **conflict**, and **slavery** was one of main **issues**. The South's **economy** depended on slavery. The North opposed slavery. Abraham Lincoln was the President of the United States when the South seceded. He felt it was necessary to keep the Union together.

At first the Union **army** was defeated many times. The northern army had many **losses**. **General** Robert E. Lee of the southern army was a very good leader. At first the Confederate army won many **victories**. Gettysburg, however, was a major **defeat** for the South. Nowadays, there are many **re-enactments** of Civil War battles. Civil War **buffs** get together with their **uniforms** and **rifles** and perform the battles again as a show.

In 1863, Gettysburg was dedicated as a National **Cemetery**. Lincoln came to Gettysburg to give a speech. His short, powerful speech became known as the Gettysburg **Address**. It is still one of the most stirring speeches ever made.

Today, the visitor to Gettysburg can walk across the battlefield and look at the many monuments that are **memorials** to the soldiers who fought and died at Gettysburg.

Exercises

C. Do you know these idioms and expressions? Work with a partner and put them in the sentences below.

this very spot	break away	broke the back
takes place	go on	a matter of time
turning point	__ after __	hold __ off
In a nutshell	turned the tide	take a look

1. The South wanted to _____ _____ from the union and become an independent country.

2. The South won battle _____ battle, and the North had loss _____ loss, until Gettysburg. At Gettysburg, the northern victory _____ _____ _____.

3. Lincoln stood on _____ _____ _____ and gave his famous speech.

4. The battle at Gettysburg was the _____ _____ in the war, and the South began to lose the battles.

5. ____ __ _____, the basic problem was slavery.

6. A re-enactment _____ _____ here every year.

7. How long did the war _____ _____?

8. After Gettysburg, it was just ___ _____ ___ _____ for the Confederacy. The end was coming.

9. The Union army was too strong, and even Lee couldn't _____ them _____.

10. The southern loss at Gettysburg _____ _____ _____ of the Confederate army. They were no longer strong and victorious.

11. Let's go and _____ ___ _____ at the battlefield monuments.

A Confederate soldier's cap, flag, and weapons

D. What do you remember? After you do the talk show, do this true or false review.

1. _____ Gettysburg was the site of a battle during the Civil War.

2. _____ At first, the Northern Army was stronger and won many battles.

3. _____ The Northern Army was defeated at Gettysburg.

4 _____ The southern states said they needed slaves.

5 _____ At Gettysburg, the Southern Army was larger.

6. _____ Robert E. Lee was a southerner.

7. _____ Gettysburg is a military cemetery.

8. _____ Gettysburg was the bloodiest battle of the war.

9 _____ Lincoln gave a speech to the soldiers at Gettysburg.

10. _____ Lincoln wrote his speech on an envelope.

Number right _____/10

E. Vocabulary Review. Finish these sentences.

1. Gettysburg is the site of a _____ War battle.

2. The South wanted to be an _____ country.

3. The Southern states _____ from the Union.

4. Abraham Lincoln was the _____ of the North.

5. Lincoln _____ the secession.

6. Robert E. Lee was a general in the _____ army.

7. At first, the South won many _____.

8. At Gettysburg, the _____ army was victorious.

9. Lincoln's speech at Gettysburg is called the _____ _____.

10. The South needed _____, but the North opposed it.

Number right _____/10

F. These adjectives are used in the talk show. Can you use them?

____ tragic	____ political	____ cautious
____ complete	____ independent	____ cultural
____ smart	____ authentic	____ economic
____ moral	____ small	____ powerful
____ social	____ weak	____ outnumbered
____ various		

G. The following is part of Lincoln's Gettysburg Address. On a separate piece of paper, write what it means to you.

. . . government of the people, by the people, for the people, shall not perish from the earth.

H. Check out one of these websites on the internet. Tell or write about something you found interesting.

www.gettysburg.com

www. nps.gov/getc/

www.nps.gov/arho/ (Robert E. Lee Memorial)

Chicago
Birthplace of the Skyscraper

A. PREVIEW. Do you know these words? Look for them in the reading below.

____ skyscraper	____ tragedy	____ architect	____ harmony
____ sidewalk	____ nightmare	____ invention	____ landscape
____ lantern	____ damage	____ elevator	____ vertigo
____ inferno	____ boom	____ girder	

B. Read this.

Chicago is a city of tall and beautiful **skyscrapers**. When you look up at them from the busy **sidewalks**, they look magnificent.

In 1871 there was a great fire in the city. The fire may have started in a barn. People say that Mrs. O'Leary's cow kicked over a **lantern** and started the fire. The fire burned for 24 hours, fanned by a strong wind. It was an **inferno**. Many people were killed in this terrible **tragedy**, and a lot of property was destroyed and thousands were left homeless. It was a **nightmare**. The city was ruined. The **damage** was enormous.

After the fire, the city rose again from its ashes and there was a huge building **boom**. Many **architects** came to design and rebuild the city. The **invention** of the **elevator** allowed the architects to construct tall buildings. One man, William LeBaron Jenney, built the world's first skyscraper. It was ten stories high. He used a framework of iron and steel **girders**.

One famous architect, Frank Lloyd Wright, designed many beautiful buildings. His buildings are in **harmony** with the natural environment and create beautiful **landscapes**.

Today the tallest building in Chicago is the Sears Tower. It is 110 stories high. If you have **vertigo**, it is not a good idea to climb to the top. The majestic and graceful skyscrapers of Chicago sit on the shore of Lake Michigan. The wind from the lake blows through the streets, and Chicago is called The Windy City.

Exercises

C. Do you know these idioms and expressions? Work with a partner and put them in the sentences below.

How about	by the time	in harmony with
kick off	in ruins	What do you say
dies hard	fielded the question	blows away
kicked up	As a matter of fact	hot air

1. Hundreds of buildings burned. The city was ____ _____ .

2. Wright's buildings are ____ _____ _____ the environment. They look so natural.

3. It's a great story and people love to tell it. It may not be true, but it _____ _____ .

4. The politician _____ _____ _____ very well. He answered clearly and directly.

5. A: Where do you want to go?
   B: _____ _____ going to Chicago?
   A: Good idea! Let's go!

6. Let's _____ _____ today's tour with a visit to the Sears Tower. The view from the top is a great way to begin.

7. A: _____ ____ _____ _____ we take a break?
   B: That's fine with me.

8. He spoke for over an hour and said nothng — just a lot of _____ _____ .

9. We won't see them because ____ _____ _____ we get to Houston, they'll be gone.

10. It was a gorgeous day until the wind _____ ____ all the dust, and it started to rain.

11. A: Do you know where the Sears Tower is?
    B : ____ __ _____ ____ _____ I do. I work there.

12. A storm is coming. Let's bring in the lawn furniture before it _____ _____ in the wind.

D. What do you remember? After you do the talk show, do this true or false review.

1. _____ Chicago burned in 1771.

2. _____ It is said that a cow started the fire.

3. _____ The fire started in a barn.

4. _____ The firemen went to the wrong place, and when they got there it was too late.

5. _____ Only a few people were killed.

6. _____ Thousands were left homeless.

7. _____ Louis Sullivan built the first skyscraper.

8. _____ The first skyscraper was only ten stories high.

9. _____ The Sears Tower is the world's tallest building.

10. _____ Chicago is located on the shore of Lake Michigan.

Number right _____/10

Chicago's Lake Michigan shoreline. The Sears Tower is to the right.

E. Vocabulary Review. Finish these sentences.

1. The first _____ was built in Chicago.

2. The fire started in a barn when a cow kicked over a _____.

Exercises

3. Jenney, Sullivan, and Wright were _____.

4. Wright's buildings were in harmony with the _____.

5. Jenney used an all-metal _____.

6. The Sears Tower is 110 _____ high.

7. Chicago is called The _____ City.

8. The fire killed 300 and made thousands _____.

9. The invention of the _____ made it possible to build tall buildings.

10. Chicago arose from its _____ like the Phoenix.

Number right _____/10

F. These adjectives are used in the talk show. Can you use them?

____ interesting	____ raging	____ majestic	____ simple
____ busy	____ absolute	____ graceful	____ essential
____ magnificent	____ exciting	____ creative	____ natural
____ enormous	____ tall	____ radical	____ close
____ gorgeous	____ high	____ unusual	____ windy

G. On a separate piece of paper, write about a building that you find interesting. Tell about its name, where it is, its purpose, and what it looks like.

H. Check out one of these websites on the internet. Tell or write about something you found interesting.

www.ci.chi.il.us/   (City of Chicago)

www.skyscraper.org   (Skyscraper Museum)

www.pbs.org/flw/   (companion to a film, *Frank Lloyd Wright*, by Ken Burns and Lynn Novick)

Exercises

St. Louis

Gateway to the West

A. PREVIEW. Do you know these words? Look for them in the reading below.

____ gateway	____ continent	____ corps	____ interpreter
____ explorer	____ waterway	____ discovery	____ arch
____ expedition	____ territory	____ canoe	____ expansion
____ pioneer	____ adventure	____ grizzly bear	
____ purchase	____ frontier		

B. Read this selection.

St. Louis is known as the **Gateway** to the West. The **explorers** Lewis and Clark began and ended their **expedition** in St. Louis, and many **pioneers** traveled to the West from here.

In 1803, President Jefferson bought a huge piece of land from France. It was called the Louisiana **Purchase**. Jefferson wanted to know more about the **continent**, its people, and its wildlife. He also wanted to know if there was a **waterway** all the way to the Pacific Ocean. He asked Meriwether Lewis to lead an expedition and explore this unknown **territory**.

Lewis asked his friend William Clark to join him. It was a dangerous and risky journey, but the two men were frontiersmen. They loved **adventure** and the opportunity to explore the **frontier**.

They left St. Louis in May 1804 with 30 men. Their expedition was called the **Corps** of **Discovery**. It was a treacherous journey as they traveled up the river in **canoes**. There were many dangers, such as **grizzly bears**. There were some unfriendly Indians, but some Indians were helpful. The young Indian woman on the expedition, Sacagawea, was a tremendous help as an **interpreter** and guide. They returned in 1806.

The Gateway **Arch** is a monument in St. Louis. It is part of the National **Expansion** Memorial to celebrate the growth of the country westward. It was designed by Eero Saarinen. It is simple, elegant, and beautiful. It represents the gateway to a new life in the West.

Exercises

C. Do you know these idioms and expressions? Work with a partner and put them in the sentences below.

In fact	take on	couldn't say enough
find out	pass ___ up	another matter
head up	took off	got together
get in touch with	bring ___ down	Would you care to

1. Lewis and Clark were the perfect men to _____ ____this dangerous expedition. They loved adventure.

2. If you get a chance to visit the arch, don't _____ it ____. It's very interesting.

3. A lot of people _____ _____ and decided to do something to celebrate the city's past.

4. I went there to _____ ___ _____ _____ an old friend who lives there.

5. Jefferson wanted to _____ _____ more about the land west of the Mississippi. It was almost unknown in those days.

6. Sacagawea was extremely valuable. Lewis and Clark _____ _____ _____ about her courage and knowledge of the country.

7. Finally, they were ready, and the expedition _____ _____ for the unknown.

8. The angry man was so big and strong, it took three men to _____ him _____.

9. Jefferson thought Lewis was the perfect man to _____ ____ the expedition.

10. We're going to St. Louis for the weekend. _____ _____ _____ ____ join us?

11. They were so happy to get to the Pacific, but staying there was _____ _____. It was so cold and wet. They hated it.

12. Lewis and Clark were gone for over two years, and there was little or no news. ____ _____, many people thought they were dead.

24   **St. Louis**

Exercises

D. What do you remember? After you do the talk show, do this true or false review.

1. _____ St. Louis is in the state of Mississippi.

2. _____ The Louisiana Purchase incuded land that later became several states.

3. _____ Clark asked Lewis to join him on the expedition.

4. _____ The purpose of the expedition was to find gold.

5. _____ The expedition left St. Louis in 1804.

6. _____ They spent a very pleasant winter on the Pacific coast.

7. _____ They returned to St. Louis a year later.

8. _____ Sacagawea left her baby in St. Louis.

9. _____ The expedition was called the Corps of Discovery.

10. _____ The arch did not close in 1993 when the Mississippi flooded the area.

Number right _____/10

*Sacajawea
with her baby*

E. Vocabulary Review. Finish these sentences.

1. St. Louis is known as the _____ to the West.

2. France owned a huge part of the _____.

3. The land was called the Louisiana _____.

4. Jefferson asked Lewis and Clark to lead the _____. It was

   called the Corps of _____

5. Sacagawea was the expedition's _____ and guide.

6. The explorers traveled by _____ on the Missouri River.

7. Many _____ left from St. Louis to settle the West.

8. Eero Saarinen was the _____ who designed the arch.

9. The arch stayed open even during the _____ in 1993.

Number right _____ / 10

F. These adjectives are used in the talk show. Can you use them?

____ delighted	____ treacherous	____ overjoyed
____ influential	____ risky	____ hostile
____ depressing	____ elegant	____ unknown
____ friendly	____ dead	____ inverted
____ dangerous	____ helpful	____ wide open
____ upside down	____ curious	____ amazing
____ exact	____ awful	

G. On a separate piece of paper write about another famous explorer. What was his name? Where did he go? When? What did he find? What was the result of his trip?

H. Check out these websites on the internet. Tell or write about something you found interesting.

www.explorestlouis.com   (St. Louis)

www.nps.gov/lecl/ (Lewis and Clark)

www.nps.gov/jeff/   (National Expansion Memorial)

Mount Rushmore

A Tribute to Four Presidents

A. PREVIEW. Do you know these words? Look for them in the reading below.

____ hills	____ models	____ stonecutter	____ fossil
____ sculpture	____ granite	____ depression	____ cave
____ preservation	____ dynamite	____ pyramid	____ prairie
____ vision			

B. Read this selection.

Mount Rushmore is located in the Black **Hills** of South Dakota. It is a remarkable **sculpture**. The heads of four presidents are carved into the side of the mountain.

The awesome sculpture is huge. The presidents' heads are 60 feet high and 20 feet wide. The sculptor was Gutzon Borglum. He chose Washington, Jefferson, Lincoln and Roosevelt. He said they represented the birth, growth, **preservation**, and development of the country. He wanted to remind the American people of America's power and greatness. For Borglum, the presidents represented America's **vision**.

Borglum first created **models** of the heads, and then the sculpture was carved into **granite**. The work was dangerous, and the workers used **dynamite**. Remarkably, no one was killed. Although the work was dangerous, the men were happy to have jobs as **stonecutters**. In 1927, there was an economic **depression** in America.

Borglum died just seven months before the work was completed, but his son completed the work in 1941. It is one of the world's largest monuments. The Great **Pyramid** in Egypt is larger.

There are other interesting places near Mount Rushmore. The eroded rock of the Badlands contains large **fossil** beds, and Wind **Cave** is an underground national park with beautiful **prairie** grasslands above ground.

Nowadays, millions of people visit Mount Rushmore every year.

Exercises

C. Do you know these idioms and expressions? Work with a partner and put them in the sentences below.

had in mind   out of work   get a kick out of
can hardly wait   As time goes by   sorry to say
ringing off the hook   got caught up in   passed away
touch and go   Among other things   call on

1. He was finally earning some money after being _____ ___ _____ for almost a year.

2. I am _____ ___ _____ I can't do that. It's simply out of the question.

3. When it happened, the phones at the police station were _____ _____ _____ _____. Everybody in town called.

4. For a while, it was _____ _____ ___, but finally the worker was rescued and out of danger.

5. He worked at many jobs. _____ _____ _____, he was employed as a stonecutter.

6. We leave for Oregon next week, but I _____ _____ _____. I'm ready to go now.

7. I don't know what she _____ ___ _____ when she did that. Who knows what she was thinking?

8. I really enjoy listening to the old man. I really _____ ___ _____ _____ ___ the way he tells stories — so amusing and colorful.

9. Her father _____ _____ while she was traveling in Italy, and she had to come home for the funeral.

10. We were going to _____ ___ the Browns when we reached Rapid City, but unfortunately, they were in Chicago.

11. As the game progressed, everybody _____ _____ ___ ___ the excitement and the tension. Would the Patriots win again?

12. ___ _____ _____ ___, my memory of those days is still strong. Neither time nor distance weakens that experience. I'll never forget it.

28   **Mount Rushmore**

Exercises

Presidents Washington, Jefferson, Roosevelt, and Lincoln on Mount Rushmore

D. What do yo remember? After you do the talk show, do this true or false review.

1. _____ Mount Rushmore is in the Black Hills of South Dakota.

2. _____ Mount Rushmore is a tribute to four presidents.

3. _____ The heads are as tall as a ten-story building.

4. _____ Borglum used models that were about five feet tall.

5. _____ Granite is a hard rock.

6. _____ The workers couldn't use dynamite.

7. _____ Several workers were killed.

8. _____ It took 24 years to complete the monument.

9. _____ Gutzon Borglum died in 1941.

10. _____ Borglum's son's name was Lincoln.

Number right _____/ 10

E. Vocabulary Review. Finish these sentences.

1. Gutzon Borglum was the _____ of Mount Rushmore.

2. The heads of four presidents are carved into the _____.

A Tribute to Four Presidents

3. The faces are 60 _____ tall.

4. The type of rock in the mountain is _____.

5. Washington represents the _____ of the country.

6. Lincoln represents the _____ of the country.

7. In 1927 there was an economic _____ in the United States.

8. The work was very _____, but no one was killed.

9. The project employed many _____.

10. The Great _____ of Egypt is larger.

Number right _____ / 10

F. These adjectives are used in the talk show. Can you use them?

____ incredible	____ noble	____ whole	____ colossal
____ glad	____ fancy	____ sure	____ underground
____ remarkable	____ hard	____ proud	____ memorable
____ awesome	____ dangerous	____ large	

G. On a separate piece of paper, write about another famous sculpture. Describe it. What is it called? What does it represent? When was it made? Where is it? Who made it? Or write about another president.

H. Check out one of these websites on the internet. Tell or write about something you found interesting.

www.mtrushmore.net   (Mount Rushmore National Monument)

www. whitehouse.gov/history/presidents (Presidents of the US)

www.nps.gov/badl (Badlands National Park)

www. nps.gov/wica   (Wind Cave National Park)

The Oregon Trail

The Way West to Fortunes and Farmlands

A. PREVIEW. Do you know these words? Look for them in the reading below.

___ trail	___ range	___ cholera	___ disease
___ fur trader	___ wagon	___ campsites	___ measles
___ pass	___ oxen	___ missionary	___ migration
___ continental divide		___ pregnant	

B. Read this selection.

The National Historic Oregon **Trail** Interpretive Center is located near Baker City, Oregon. It tells the story of the pioneers who traveled the trail about 150 years ago. The trail is about 2000 miles long.

Before 1811, the British controlled Oregon Territory, but American **fur traders** were beginning to work in the territory. They built Astoria, Oregon and named it after John Jacob Astor. One of his ships was lost at sea, and a group of men headed back to Missouri to report the loss. Robert Stuart led the group and discovered the South **Pass** through the mountains of the **continental divide**, just south of the Wind River **Range** in Wyoming.

When Captain Bonneville crossed the pass with **wagons**, ordinary people realized they could move west with wagons. Over 300,000 people made the long journey in wagons pulled by **oxen**. They were going to the rich farmland of the Williamette Valley in Oregon.

It was a hard and dangerous journey. At least 30,000 died along the way. Most of the deaths were because of accidents and disease — especially **cholera**. The **campsites** along the trail were very dirty and the water was often contaminated.

Doctor Marcus Whitman was a **missionary** who wanted to set up a mission in the West and bring Christianity to the Indians. He and his **pregnant** wife traveled the trail and established a mission in Walla Walla, Washington. Unfortunately, many Indians died from a **disease** – the **measles.** They thought the Whitmans had poisoned them, and they killed them.

The **migration** was made by about 300,000 people, and about 30,000 died along the way. The trail brought two cultures into conflict, and in the end, the culture of the settlers prevailed.

Exercises

C. Do you know these idioms and expressions? Work with a partner and put them in the sentences below.

on our doorstep   so to speak   on your mind
thumbnail sketch   pointed out   went off
boiled down   word spread   in short
move in   as well as   time was up

1. Fur traders and pioneers, ____ _____ ____ missionaries, followed the trail.

2. The _____ _____ quickly, and soon thousands heard that it was possible to take wagons on the trail.

3. The result was, ____ _____, thousands took a chance and headed west.

4. The Indians were not very happy when the settlers began to _____ ____ and take the land.

5. All this happened just a few miles from here, almost ____ _____ _____.

6. Too often, a loaded gun _____ _____ accidentally and killed someone.

7. When the bear attacked, he thought his _____ _____ ____ and he didn't have a chance.

8. I think you have something ____ _____ _____. Tell me about it.

9. We thought it would be easy to cross the river here, but our guide _____ _____ that it was too deep in the middle.

10. For some settlers, the danger and the hardship was, ____ ____ _____, one long nightmare.

11. How can I give you a _____ _____ of the history of this trail? There's just too much to tell.

12. The causes of death can be _____ _____ to two things: accidents and disease.

Exercises

D. What do you remember? After you do the talk show, do this true or false review.

1. _____ The Oregon Trail begins in St. Louis.

2. _____ The trail is about 2,000 miles long.

3. _____ Astoria was a British fort.

4. _____ Stuart realized that wagons could make it through the South Pass.

5. _____ The South Pass is in Missouri.

6. _____ Captain Bonneville discovered the South Pass.

7. _____ There is a dam on the Columbia River named after Bonneville.

8. _____ Many settlers died by drinking contaminated water.

9. _____ The Whitman Mission was destroyed by cholera.

10. _____ Narcissa Whitman went all the way to Portland.

Number right _____/10

Reproduction of a prairie schooner

E. Vocabulary Review. Finish these sentences.

1. Thousands of _____ pulled by oxen passed by this place.

2. They moved along at only about two _____ per _____.

3. Astoria was a fur trading post at the mouth of the Columbia _____.

4. The mountains of the continental _____ were a huge barrier.

The Way West to Fortunes and Farmlands

Exercises

5. Robert Stuart discovered the South _____.

6. Dr. Marcus Whitman was a _____.

7. The Whitmans established a _____ at Walla Walla.

8. The settlers headed for the rich farmland of the Williamette _____.

9. The terrible disease _____ killed thousands.

10. The Indians did not have immunity to the _____ the pioneers and settlers brought with them.

Number right _____/10

Prairie schooners on the Oregon Trail

F. These adjectives are used in the talk show. Can you use them?

____ interpretive	____ comfortable	____ pregnant	____ clear
____ local	____ flat	____ loaded	____ careful
____ fascinated	____ lost	____ dreaded	____ sad
____ thrilled	____ belated	____ contaminated	____ sensational

G. On a separate piece of paper, write about the longest trip you have ever taken. Where did you go? How did you travel? How long did it take? Who did you go with? Why did you go?

H. Check out one of these websites on the internet. Tell or write about something you found interesting.

http://oregontrail.blm.gov (National Historic Oregon Trail Interpretive Center)

www.endoftheoregontrail.org (End of the Oregon Trail)

www.nps.gov/whmi (Whitman Mission)

Alaska

Big and Beautiful

A. PREVIEW. Do you know these words? Look for them in the reading below.

____ glacier	____ seal	____ cartoon	____ misery
____ wildlife	____ otter	____ gold strike	____ hiker
____ strait	____ icebox	____ prospector	____ tourism
____ voyage	____ folly	____ stampede	____ Arctic Circle

B. Read this selection.

Alaska is the largest state in size. It is also a beautiful state. It has America's highest mountain, largest **glacier,** and incredible **wildlife**. In the language of the native Aleut people, Alaska means "great land."

An explorer, Vitus Bering, was perhaps the first European to discover Alaska. First he discovered the **strait** that separates Russia and Alaska. On another **voyage** he discovered the Alaskan coast. Russians moved in and began a profitable fur trade. The fur of the **seals** and **otters** was very valuable.

In 1867 Russia needed money and the fur trade was no longer so profitable. So Russia sold Alaska to the United States. William Seward was the Secretary of State who made the deal. Many people thought he was crazy. They called the land "Seward's **Icebox**," and "Seward's **Folly**." There were many **cartoons** in the newspapers making fun of Seward.

In 1896 there was a **gold strike**, and in just a few years the population doubled. Thousands of **prospectors** came, hoping to strike it rich. The gold rush became a **stampede**. But many prospectors found only **misery** in Alaska's wild mountains and cold, snowy weather. Today the "Trail of Misery" is a trail for **hikers**.

Nowadays fishing and oil are very important to Alaska, but the great natural scenery and wildlife make **tourism** very important. There are eight national parks with millions of lakes, thousands of glaciers and islands, and incredible wildlife. In the northern part of Alaska, above the **Arctic Circle**, there is daylight all day in the summer.

Exercises

C. Do you know these idioms and expressions? Work with a partner and put them in the sentences below.

not to mention   get rid of   no picnic
right away   make fun of   on top of all that
How come   pipe dream   took _____ for every cent
bottom fell out of   striking it rich   turned into

1. A: I decided to cut my vacation short.
   B: _____ _____?
   A: I ran out of money.

2. The whole village has been restored and _____ _____ a museum.

3. His hopes of _____ ____ _____ came to an unhappy end. There was no gold in the river after all.

4. There's so much to do here: hiking, rafting, kayaking, camping, _____ ____ _____ wildlife viewing.

5. Let me tell you, kayaking on this river is ____ _____. It's difficult and dangerous.

6. Everything got wet, and ____ _____ ___ _____ _____, I lost the camera.

7. You've got too much stuff in your pack. You've got to _____ _____ ____ something, and leave it in the car.

8. We were lucky. After we called, help came _____ _____ and fixed the problem.

9. Please don't _____ _____ ___ him. He's very sensitive, and laughing at him won't be helpful. It will only hurt.

10. His trip to Alaska was just a _____ _____, after all. He didn't have the time or the money.

11. He gave them his bank account number and they _____ him _____ _____ _____ he had.

12. When people stopped buying fur coats, the _____ _____ _____ ___ the fur market, and he lost everything.

36   **Alaska**

Exercises

D. What do you remember? After you do the talk show, do this true or false review.

1. _____ The highest mountain in North America is in Alaska.

2. _____ Alaska belonged to Canada in 1867.

3. _____ Many people thought Seward was crazy to buy the land.

4. _____ Denali is the only national park in Alaska.

5. _____ 75% of the population is Native Alaskan or Inuit.

6. _____ Russia needed money to pay off its losses in the Crimean War.

7. _____ Bering discovered gold in Alaska.

8. _____ Between 1890 and 1900, the population doubled.

9. _____ Tourism is the most important industry nowadays.

10. _____ Alaska is larger in size than Texas

Number right _____/ 10

E. Vocabulary Review. Finish these sentences.

1. Vitus Bering was a Danish _____.

2. Otter and seal _____ was very valuable.

3. The Russians established fur _____ posts in Alaska.

4. In 1867, William Seward was Secretary of _____.

5. Seward bought Alaska for two cents an _____.

6. Gold was _____ and thousands of _____ came to Alaska.

7. Today you can hike the "_____ of Misery."

Exercises

8. After fishing and oil, _____ is the most important business.

9. Many Eskimos prefer to be called _____, which means "the people."

Number right ____/10

Glacier in Alaska

F. These adjectives are used in the talk show. Can you use them?

____ gorgeous   ____ luxurious   ____ hardy   ____ principal
____ fascinating ____ virtual   ____ miserable   ____ stupendous
____ grand   ____ sheer   ____ greedy   ____ true
____ cold   ____ wild   ____ rough

G. If you had the opportunity to go to Alaska, what would you like to see and do, and why would you want to do it? On a separate piece of paper, write about your trip.

H. Check out one of these websites on the internet. Take notes and report on your visit.

www.denali.national-park.com (Denali National Park)

www.state.ak.us (State of Alaska)

www.kcls.org/hh/klondike.cfm (Alaskan Gold Rush)

Hawaii
The Aloha State

A. PREVIEW. Do you know these words? Look for them in the reading below.

____ volcano	____ monarchy	____ reign	____ apology
____ vegetation	____ kingdom	____ whaler	____ overthrow
____ paradise	____ heir	____ sugarcane	____ beach
____ Polynesians	____ throne	____ pineapple	____ lava
			____ surfing

B. Read this selection.

There are eight major islands in the state of Hawaii. They have beautiful beaches, active **volcanoes**, waterfalls, and wonderful flowers and **vegetation**. It's an island **paradise**.

The first Hawaiians came from the Marquesas Islands, 2000 miles away. Nowadays the population is a mixture of many different people. There are **Polynesians**, Asians, Whites, and Blacks, but no group has a majority.

In 1795, Kamehameha I united the people of Hawaii and established a **monarchy**. The **kingdom** continued for over 100 years. There were five King Kamehamehas. The Kamehamea dynasty ended when Kamehamea V did not have an **heir**. Queen Lililuokalani was the last monarch. She came to the **throne** in 1891, but two years later the monarchy was overthrown. Her **reign** did not last very long.

Captain James Cook, the great British explorer, discovered the Hawaiian Islands in 1778, and by 1820 outsiders began to arrive. There were **whalers**, businessmen, traders, and missionaries. Christian missionaries tried to change the traditions of the people. American businessmen took over the island and established a republic. Fortunes were made in **sugarcane** and **pineapples**, and finally, in 1959, Hawaii became the 50th state. In 1998, President Clinton signed an **apology** to the Hawaiian people for the **overthrow** of the monarchy.

There are many things to see in Hawaii. On the eight major islands you can see black **beaches** and bubbling **lava** in volcanoes, and the **surfing** is wonderful.

Exercises

C. Do you know these idioms and expressions? Work with a partner and put them in the sentences below.

trade places	the scoop	Better late than never
take ___ up on	a foothold	As you know
settle down	took over	one at a time
wiped out	make sure	go back

1. The disease spread rapidly and almost _____ _____ the entire village.

2. Americans finally _____ _____ the islands and established a republic.

3. They visited all the islands, _____ ____ __ _____, spending a few days on each one.

4. My vacation was over, but I didn't want to ____ _____ to snow and ice.

5. They fell in love with the place and decided to buy a home and _____ _____ there.

6. Let's _____ _____. I'll drive for a while and you can sleep.

7. A: What's _____ _____ ? What's happening?
   B: You don't know? No surfing. The beach is closed. Sharks!

8. Well, you almost missed the party, but come on in. _____ _____ _____ _____.

9. So, you stayed on Oahu. ____ _____ _____, that's where Pearl Harbor is. Did you visit the memorial?

10. When you head for the beach tomorrow, _____ _____ you have your sunglasses. It's going to be very sunny.

11. After they established __ _____, they began to expand their pineapple and sugarcane production.

12. Thanks for the offer to show us the volcanoes. We'll _____ you ____ ____ that. Where and when do we meet?

Hawaiian Coast

D. What do you remember? After you do the talk show, do this true or false review.

1. _____ The native Hawaiians are about half of the population.

2. _____ A British explorer discovered the islands.

3. _____ The first king of Hawaii was Kamehameha I.

4. _____ Kamehameha founded the Republic of Hawaii.

5. _____ Kamehameha V did not have any children.

6. _____ The missionaries taught the Hawaiians how to read and write.

7. _____ Queen Liliuokalani was the last Hawaiian monarch.

8. _____ The principal crop is bananas.

9. _____ President Clinton signed a formal apology to the Hawaiian people.

10. _____ Oahu is the biggest island.

Number right _____/10

E. Vocabulary Review. Finish these sentences.

1. I think it is _____. Heaven on earth!

2. The original people of Hawaii were _____.

Exercises

3. Kamehameha I founded the _____ of Hawaii.

4. _____ tried to change the culture of the Hawaiians.

5. They _____ the hula dance.

6. "_____" is a Hawaiian greeting or goodbye.

7. Liliuokalani rewrote the _____.

8. Her _____ was overthrown.

9. Dole became president of the _____ of Hawaii.

10. Hawaii's big island has _____ volcanoes and black beaches.

Number right _____/10

F. These adjectives are used in the talk show. Can you use them?

____ heavenly	____ perfect	____ correct	____ metropolitan
____ lush	____ native	____ inevitable	____ active
____ perfumed	____ original	____ serious	____ bubbling
____ sandy	____ isolated	____ formal	____ common
____ fantastic			

G. In 1893 the monarchy was overthrown in Hawaii. On a separate piece of paper, write about a time in another country's history when there was a change in government. When was it? Who was in power? Who took over? Did the people benefit from this change?

H. Check out these websites on the internet. Take notes below and report on your visit to your class.

www.gohawaii.com   (Hawaii travel)

www.nps.gov/havo   (Hawaiian Volcanoes National Park)

www. co.honolulu.hi.us   (Honolulu)

Exercises

The Golden Gate Bridge
San Francisco's Famous Landmark

A. PREVIEW. Do you know these words? Look for them in the reading below.

____ gate	____ tower	____ structure	____ pedestrian
____ surroundings	____ cable	____ lighting	____ jogger
____ bay	____ engineer	____ glow	____ prison
____ suspension bridge	____ current	____ illusion	____ criminal

B. Read this selection.

The Golden **Gate** Bridge in San Francisco is one of the largest and most beautiful bridges in the world. The bridge is actually orange in color, but It blends very well with the natural **surroundings**. The bridge crosses the entrance to a large **bay**. The narrow entrance to the bay was called the Golden Strait, and for that reason, the bridge is called the Golden **Gate**.

It is a **suspension bridge**. Two **towers** carry two large **cables** across the strait. The roadway is suspended from the cables. Building the bridge was a real challenge for the **engineers**. It is over a mile long, and there is a strong **current** in the water under the bridge

During construction, the workers wore hard hats and there was a net under the bridge. Although men fell off the bridge, they were caught in the net. No one was killed during the construction.

The bridge is a unique **structure**.The design of the bridge catches the sunlight and the towers look like they are very tall. At night, the **lighting** gives the bridge a special **glow**. The openings in the towers create an **illusion** that the towers are taller than they really are. During the day, the orange color of the bridge blends with the natural environment. **Pedestrians** and **joggers** enjoy crossing the bridge.

There are many interesting places in San Francisco. For example, the infamous **prison** Alcatraz is in San Francisco Bay. Many well-known **criminals** were imprisoned there. Nowadays it is a museum.

Exercises

C. Do you know these idioms and expressions? Work with a partner and put them in the sentences below.

come about	bring __ up	looks as if
came upon	cleared __ up	stick around
as the story goes	changed my mind	take it all in
get it	came up with	to name a few

1. I was going to stay in Hawaii, but I _____ ____ _____and came back to San Francisco.

2. The view from the bridge is wonderful, and you should _____ _____ for the sunset when it's really beautiful.

3. There's so much to see. It's hard to _____ ____ _____ ____ in just a few minutes.

4. So, ____ _____ _____ _____, he named the strait after the Golden Horn.

5. There's so much to see: Fisherman's Wharf, Alcatraz, the cable cars, Nob Hill, just ____ _____ ___ _____ possibilities.

6. I didn't think we could do it, but he _____ ____ _____ a great plan, and we did it.

7. Why did he do that? I don't _____ ____. I just don't understand him.

8. Bring an umbrella. It _____ ____ ____ it's going to rain.

9. I don't want to talk about it, so please don't _____ it ____ again.

10. The beaches in Hawaii were black. How did that _____ _____?

11. I was confused, but her explanation _____ everything ____. Now I get it.

12. While sailing down the coast, he _____ _____ the bay.

D. What do you remember? After you do the talk show, do this true or false review.

1. _____ The Golden Strait is in Istanbul.

2. _____ The bridge's color is international orange.

3. _____ The bridge was completed in 1897.

4. _____ You can see San Francisco from the bridge.

5. _____ San Francisco Bay is connected to the Pacific Ocean.

6. _____ Nineteen workers fell off the bridge into the bay.

7. _____ There are three tall towers holding up the roadway.

8. _____ People can walk across the bridge.

9. _____ John C. Fremont designed the bridge.

10. _____ Alcatraz is on an island in the bay.

Number right _____/10

E. Vocabulary Review. Finish these sentences.

1. The architect decided that orange would _____ with the natural setting.

2. Fremont named the entrance to the bay the Golden _____.

3. The Golden Gate is a _____ bridge.

4. There are two _____ that hold up two steel _____.

5. Lots of _____ and joggers cross the bridge.

6. It was completed ahead of _____ and under _____.

Exercises

7. San Francisco is called the City by the _____.

8. The bridge is over a _____ long.

Number right _____/10

San Francisco

F. These adjectives are used in the talk show. Can you use them?

____ spectacular	____ treacherous	____ injured	____ unique
____ incredible	____ vertical	____ majestic	____ subtle
____ real	____ difficult	____ artistic	____ infamous

G. On a separate piece of paper, write a short story about an event that happens on a bridge.

H. Check out these websites on the internet. Take notes below and report on your visit to your class.

www.nps.gov/goga   (Golden Gate Recreation Area)

www.goldengatebridge.org   (The Bridge)

www.sanfrancisco.com   (Complete Guide to San Francisco)

www.sfchinatown.com   (Chinatown)

The Golden Gate Bridge

The Grand Canyon
America's Great Natural Wonder

A. PREVIEW. Do you know these words? Look for them in the reading below.

____ canyon   ____ crew   ____ natural resources

____ reservation   ____ exhaustion   ____ congress

____ creek   ____ triumph   ____ rafting

____ geology   ____ conquerer   ____ mule

____ rapids   ____ conservation

B. Read this selection and underline any words you're not sure of. Write them below and find out what they mean.

The Grand **Canyon** is in the state of Arizona. It is an enormous canyon — 227 miles long, one mile deep, and 18 miles across. The Colorado River formed the canyon. The size and the colors of the canyon are grand.

Years ago, various Indians lived in the canyon. Even today the Havasupai Indians have a **reservation** on a **creek** at the bottom of the canyon.

The first man to fully explore the canyon was John Wesley Powell. He was a professor of **geology**. In 1869, he and a small group of men took boats through the canyon. There were many waterfalls and **rapids**. It took Powell and his **crew** 98 days. They lost three men on the way. It was a harrowing adventure. At the end they were almost dead from **exhaustion**, but the adventure was a **triumph**, and Powell was called the "**Conquerer** of the Colorado."

President Theodore Roosevelt was very interested in **conservation**. He wanted to protect America's **natural resources**. He helped protect the canyon. **Congress** made it a national park in 1919. Today, many tourists visit it. People can go hiking or go **rafting** in the canyon, or even ride a **mule** down to the bottom.

Exercises

C. Do you know these idioms and expressions? Work with a partner and put them in the sentences below.

getting ahead of myself	on edge	and all
put __ into words	take __ chances	speaking of
Now you're talking	did __ in	call __ up
put __ on the map	walk in the park	better off

1. Crossing the river here won't be easy, but I'll _____ my _____. I think I can do it.

2. The hike today almost _____ me ___. I can't take another step.

3. We lost everything, packs _____ _____.

4. Let me try to _____ it _____ _____. It's an incredible, majestic, awesome, gorgeous place. You've got to see it to believe it.

5. When you're in town again, _____ me ___, and we'll have dinner together.

6. River rafting has _____ this little town ___ _____ _____. It's really busy now.

7. Let me tell you, we were all ___ _____, waiting to hear the news. Every one was tense.

8. It used to be difficult and dangerous. Now, it's just a _____ ___ _____ _____ — very easy.

9. But I'm _____ _____ ___ _____. Let me go back to the beginning of the story.

10. The adventures of Lewis and Clark were amazing, and _____ ___ adventure, Powell's trip down the Colorado was really something.

11. Let's stop here and get something to eat. _____ _____ _____! I'm really hungry.

12. Well, I think you'd be _____ _____ just staying at home and resting. We can see the canyon tomorrow, when you're feeling better.

D. What do you remember? After you do the talk show, do this true or false review.

1. _____ The colors of the canyon change during the day.

2. _____ Indians did not live in the canyon.

3. _____ Powell had been a soldier during the Civil War.

4. _____ Powell started out with over a hundred men.

5. _____ It took three weeks for Powell to travel through the canyon.

6. _____ They traveled down the river on rafts.

7. _____ Three of Powell's men tried to get out of the canyon.

8. _____ There were many waterfalls on the river.

9. _____ There was no gold in the canyon.

10. _____ Theodore Roosevelt established the canyon as a national park.

Number right _____/10

The Grand Canyon of the Colorado River

Exercises

E. Vocabulary Review. Finish these sentences.

1. The Grand Canyon is 227 miles long, one mile _____, and 18 miles _____.

2. The Havasupai Indians live on a small _____ in the Canyon.

3. There are many waterfalls and _____ in the Colorado River.

4. Powell was a _____ of geology.

5. Prospectors didn't find _____ but they did find some other _____.

6. Roosevelt is known as the _____ president.

7. Today you can go _____ down the river.

8. Today, the canyon is a _____ park.

Number right _____/10

F. These adjectives are used in the talk show. Can you use them?

____ awesome	____ favorite	____ wooden	____ modern
____ enormous	____ fast	____ ferocious	____ inaccessible
____ deep	____ exciting	____ grim	____ valuable
____ disappointed	____ harrowing		

G. On a separate piece of paper, write about a natural landscape that you are familiar with. What is its name? Where is it? What can you see and do there?

H. Check out these websites on the internet. Take notes below and report on your visit.

www.nps.gov/grca   (Grand Canyon National Park)

www.azstarnet.com/grandcanyonriver   (River running)

www.havasupaitribe.com   (Havasupai Indians)

The Grand Canyon

Exercises

Mesa Verde
Home of the Ancient Anasazi

A. PREVIEW. Do you know these words? Look for them in the reading below.

____ landmark   ____ artifact   ____ ladder   ____ council
____ tribe   ____ pottery   ____ dwelling   ____ cermony
____ plateau   ____ cliff   ____ drought   ____ elders
____ archeologist   ____ shelf   ____ palace   ____ descendants
____ pueblo

B. Read this selection.

A well-known **landmark** in the state of Colorado is Mesa Verde, a national park in the state of Colorado. It was the home of an ancient Indian **tribe**, the Anasazi. They lived on the high **plateaus** (mesas) for over a thousand years. **Archeologists** have found many **artifacts** that show that the Anaszi made beautiful **pottery** and baskets. They left the area sometime in the 1300s and moved south to New Mexico and Arizona.

The Anasazi built villages in the side of **cliffs**. They sit on a **shelf** in the cliff and are reached by **ladders**. The Anasazi only lived in these cliff **dwellings** for about 200 years, and then they moved away. It is thought that a long **drought** made it difficult to grow food, and they had to leave. One village of cliff dwellings in the side of the cliff still exists for visitors at Mesa Verde. It is called "The Cliff **Palace**."

An important part of the village was the "kiva." It was a large **council** room where people discussed community matters. It was also used for religious **ceremonies**. In this ancient culture, **elders** were very important, and young people looked up to them.

The Anasazi do not exist now. Their **descendants** became the **Pueblo** Indians. The Pueblo include the Hopi of Arizona, the Zuñi, and Taos of New Mexico. The word "pueblo" also means "village" in Spanish and English.

Exercises

C. Do you know these idioms and expressions? Work with a partner and put them in the sentences below.

In other words	pulled up	talk ___ over
if I may	moved away	simply put
get up	had no choice	looked up to
get down	as far as we know dug up	dug up

1. After the flood, several families _____ _____ and went to live on higher ground.

2. Let me add, ____ ___ _____, another interesting point.

3. Let's _____ it _____ before we make a decision.

4. He did a lot of research and _____ ____ several interesting facts.

5. How did you _____ ____ to the top so fast? Wasn't it difficult?

6. A: It was beautiful, so we stayed there for several days.
   B: ____ _____ _____, you really liked it there.

7. There were many reasons for their decision to leave, but _____ _____, they were hungry.

8. I have always _____ _____ _____ her. She was a great teacher and a wonderful person. I admire and respect her.

9. The cat climbed up the tree and couldn't _____ _____. I had to go up and get it.

10. After their boat sank, they got some ropes and _____ it ____ to the surface.

11. We ____ ____ _____. We simply couldn't go on because we had lost all our equipment.

12. No one is sure, but ____ _____ ____ ___ _____, they lived on the mesa for a long time — perhaps a thousand years.

Exercises

Cliff dwellings of the Anasazi

D. What do you remember? After you do the talk show, do this true or false review.

1. _____ Mesa Verde is located in Colorado.

2. _____ Mesa Verde is a national park.

3. _____ Mesa is a French word.

4. _____ The Anasazi lived on Mesa Verde for 200 years.

5. _____ The Anasazi left Mesa Verde in the eighteenth century.

6. _____ The descendants of the Anaszi now live in Arizona and New Mexico.

7. _____ There are many floods during a drought.

8. _____ The Taos Indians live in Texas.

9. _____ A mesa is a kind of plateau.

10. _____ The Hopi and Zuñi are Pueblo Indians.

Number right ____/10

Home of the Ancient Anasazi

Exercises

E. Vocabulary Review. Finish these sentences.

1. The Spanish word for "table" is " _____ ."

2. The Anasazi were an ancient Indian _____ .

3. The Pueblo Indians are _____ of the Anaszi.

4. They used _____ to get up and down the cliffs.

5. The cliff _____ were built on a shelf in the side of a cliff.

6. The _____ lasted for 24 years — a long time with little rain.

7. _____ have dug up a lot of pottery.

8. They were known as "The _____ People" because of their beautiful _____ .

9. The _____ Indians live in Arizona.

10. In these cultures, young people looked up to their _____ .

Number right ____/10

F. These adjectives are used in the talk show. Can you use them?

____ amazing	____ appropriate	____ strange	____ religious
____ mountainous	____ unusual	____ terrible	____ handcrafted
____ ancient	____ dangerous	____ thriving	____ proud

G. Find out about an American Indian tribe and write about them on a separate piece of paper. Where do they live? What is their history? What are they famous for?

H. Check out these websites on the internet. Take notes and report on your visit to your class.

www.nps.gov/meve   (Mesa Verde National Park)

http://mo.essortment.com/pueblowherecan_riij.htm   (Pueblo Indians)

www.state.co.us   (State of Colorado)

Exercises

Remember the Alamo!

Texas' War for Independence

A. PREVIEW. Do you know these words? Look for them in the reading below.

____ mission	____ dictator	____ colonel	____ treaty
____ monastery	____ constitution	____ reinforcements	____ rancher
____ fort	____ rebel	____ ammunition	____ cattle
____ independence	____ revenge		

A. Read this selection.

The Alamo is a **mission** in San Antonio, Texas. A mission was a church and a **monastery** surrounded by walls. It was built by the Spanish to spread Christianity in the New World. In the war between Texas and Mexico, it was used as a **fort** by the Texans.

Until 1835, Texas was part of Mexico. Mexico had recently won **independence** from Spain and were led by a strong **dictator**, Santa Anna, who had suspended the **constitution**. However, many Americans had moved into Texas. The Americans decided they wanted to be independent of Mexico. The Mexican government, led by the dictator, General Santa Anna, did not want Texas to become independent. The Mexicans considered the Americans to be **rebels**. After the Americans attacked a Mexican village, Santa Anna wanted **revenge**. The result was war — the Texas Revolution.

The Alamo became the site of a battle between the Mexican army and a small number of Americans commanded by **Colonel** Travis. The Americans used the Alamo as a fort. The Americans were surrounded by an army led by General Santa Anna. The Americans could not escape. They expected **reinforcements**, but they never came, and after a while they ran out of **ammunition**. All of the American defenders in the fort were killed.

After the Alamo, the Texans, led by Sam Houston, defeated the Mexicans and captured Santa Anna. They forced Mexico to sign a **treaty** and Texas became independent. Later, in 1845, Texas became a state.

There is much to see in San Antonio. There are four other missions on the Mission Trail. Another trail, the Chisholm Trail, was important in San Antonio's history. On this trail, **ranchers** sent their **cattle** north to the railroad and on to the markets.

Today, San Antonio is the best of two worlds: American and Mexican.

Exercises

C. Do you know these idioms and expressions? Work with a partner and put them in the sentences below.

not about to	showed up	get out
iron hand	hold out	beefed up
push __ around	give up	go after
tells it like it is	pinned down	time heals all wounds

1. The enemy army began to retreat, so the rebels decided to ____ _____ them while they were weak.

2. When the reinforcements finally _____ _____ it was too late. The battle was over.

3. The _____ _____ of the dictator finally weakened, and the people began to rebel.

4. They had to _____ ____. They had no choice. Continuing to fight was hopeless.

5. We were _____ _____; we couldn't move. The enemy fire was very heavy.

6. Some men wanted to _____ _____ of the fort, but it was impossible to leave.

7. After they _____ ____ their army, they were stronger and ready to attack.

8. She always _____ ____ _____ ____ ____: directly, honestly, and openly.

9. No, I am _____ _____ ____ do that. It's a bad idea, and I won't do it.

10. "Don't try to _____ me _____," he said. I'm not afraid of you.

11. Do you really think _____ _____ _____ _____? Some people never seem to forgive and forget.

12. They ran out of ammunition and couldn't _____ _____ any longer.

                                               Remember the Alamo!

Exercises

D. What do you remember? After you do the talk show, do this true or false review.

1. _____ The Alamo is in Houston, Texas.

2. _____ Santa Anna was the Mexican commander.

3. _____ William Travis became the governor of Texas.

4. _____ Texas was originally part of Mexico.

5. _____ At one time, Mexico was controlled by Spain.

6. _____ Nobody got out of the Alamo.

7. _____ Davy Crockett was the commander at the Alamo.

8. _____ Eighteen Americans died at the Alamo.

9. _____ Texas was an independent country until 1910.

10. _____ The Alamo was completely destroyed in the battle.

Number right _____/10

E. Vocabulary Review. Finish these sentences.

1. The Alamo ws originally built as a _____.

2. The purpose of the mission was to spread _____.

3. The Americans wanted to be _____.

4. Santa Anna was the Mexican general and _____.

5. The Mexicans considered the Americans to be _____.

6. The men of the Alamo expected _____.

7. They ran out of _____.

8. "_____ the Alamo," was their battle cry.

9. Sam Houston was the _____ of the Texas army.

10. Texas was an independent _____ for about ten years.

Number right _____/10

The Alamo,
San Antonio, Texas

F. These adjectives are used in the talk show. Can you use them?

____ historic	____ historical	____ confident	____ wild
____ surrounding	____ necessary	____ outnumbered	____ independent
____ particular	____ illegal	____ trusted	____ countless

G. You are a reporter. On a separate piece of paper, write about a famous battle that you know about. Where was it? When did it happen? Who was involved? Who won? What happened after?

H. Check out these websites on the internet. Take notes and report on your visit to your class.

www.thealamo.org (The Alamo)

www.state.tx.us (State of Texas)

www.mexonline.com (Mexico)

New Orleans

A Cultural Mélange

A. PREVIEW. Do you know these words? Look for them in the reading below.

____ Creole	____ Lent	____ sauce	____ jazz
____ Cajun	____ fast	____ spice	____ trumpet
____ Mardi Gras	____ Easter	____ gourmet	____ riverboats
____ festival	____ parades	____ concerts	

B. Read this selection and underline any words you're not sure of. Write them below and find out what they mean.

New Orleans, Louisiana, is a city with a wonderful ethnic mix. There are descendants of the French and Spanish settlers. They are called **Creoles**. There are **Cajuns** — French Canadians who were originally from Nova Scotia, Canada. There are many African-Americans, and many others from Europe and Latin America.

Mardi Gras is a huge **festival** that happens every year. It is called "fat Tuesday" because it is the last day before **Lent**. Lent is the traditional beginning of a **fast** in the Christian religion. It is the last day to eat well and have fun. The fasting ends at **Easter**. Millions come for the great party. There are many **parades**, and a lot of music.

New Orleans is also famous for its great food. There are two traditions: Creole and Cajun, and each tradition features cooking with a variety of **sauces** and **spices**. Throughout New Orleans there are many fine restaurants with **gourmet** dishes.

New Orleans is famous for its music. You can hear it everywhere. There are **concerts** every night. **Jazz** was born in New Orleans. One of the great jazz musicians was Louis Armstrong. He learned to play the **trumpet** at a home for boys, and played on **riverboats** on the Mississippi River. Later he became famous all around the world.

Exercises

C. Do you know these idioms and expressions? Work with a partner and put them in the sentences below.

That is to say	get going	hooked on
all over	way back	Of all the
put on	had a ball	can't beat
let loose	get started	call it quits

1. My brother is really _____ ____ jazz; that's all he ever listens to.

2. That club really _____ ____ a great show — wonderful music and dancing and great comedy.

3. I've been _____ _____ the world, and this seafood is the best I've ever eaten.

4. Mardi Gras was a wonderful experience. _____ ____ ____ _____, I really enjoyed it

5. That song is a real oldie. It goes _____ _____.

6. A: How did you _____ _____ in pottery?
   B: As a child I enjoyed playing in the mud.

7. At the beginning of the festival, they _____ _____ thousands of balloons that sailed up into the sky.

8. For a great dessert, you _____ _____ her strawberry cheesecake.

9. Why did I say that? ____ _____ _____ dumb things to say, that was the dumbest.

10. It was a great trip. We really enjoyed it and the kids _____ ___ _____.

11. C'mon! Let's _____ _____. We're already late.

12. It's five o'clock — time to _____ ____ _____.

Exercises

D. What do you remember? After you do the talk show, do this true or false review.

1. _____ Mardi Gras is French for "Fat Tuesday."

2. _____ Mardi Gras usually takes place in the fall.

3. _____ The festivities begin several days before Tuesday.

4. _____ New Orleans is famous for its Latin American and Mexican food.

5. _____ The Cajuns arrived in New Orleans in the twentieth century.

6. _____ Gumbo is a famous New Orleans restaurant.

7. _____ Cajun cooking is spicy.

8. _____ Louis Armstrong grew up in New Orleans.

9. _____ New Orleans is on the Missouri River.

10. _____ There's a concert at Preservation Hall every night.

Number right _____/10

E. Vocabulary Review. Finish these sentences.

1. New Orleans is a wonderful _____ mix of people.

2. It's special and unusual; it's _____.

3. _____ _____ means "Fat Tuesday." It's one giant _____.

4. _____ refers to the descendants of the French and Spanish.

5. Restaurants in New Orleans offer _____ dishes.

6. The style of music called _____ was born in New Orleans

7. Louis Armstrong played the _____.

8. You can attend a _____ at Preservation Hall.

9. You can see Old World architecture in the _____ Quarter.

Number right _____/10

A street scene in the New Orleans French Quarter

F. These adjectives are used in the talk show. Can you use them?

____ unique	____ spectacular	____ delicious	____ poor
____ ethnic	____ giant	____ elegant	____ integrated
____ exotic	____ fine	____ spicy	____ live
____ free	____ thick	____ sweet	

G. On a separate piece of paper, write about one of these topics.
   a. My favorite festival.
   b. The food of _____ (country or ethnic group).
   c. Why I like _____ (kind of music).

H. Check out these websites on the internet. Take notes and report on your visit to your class.

www.neworleansonline.com   (New Orleans)

www. allaboutjazz.com   (jazz)

www.mardigras.com   (Mardi Gras)

www.gumbopages.com/recipe-page.html   (Creole and Cajun recipes)

The Kennedy Space Center
The Exploration of Space

A. PREVIEW. Do you know these words? Look for them in the reading below.

____ space	____ vehicle	____ launching pad	____ disaster
____ spacecraft	____ assembly	____ operations	____ universe
____ program	____ shuttle	____ orbit	____ curiosity
____ astronaut			

B. Read this selection and underline the words you're not sure of. Write them below and find out what they mean.

The Kennedy **Space** Center is located on Cape Canaveral on the east coast of Florida. It is a huge place where NASA launches **spacecraft**. The center was built in 1950, and has launched over 3,000 spacecraft. The Mercury **Program** was the first US project to send an **astronaut** into space.

The space center is huge. There is the **vehicle assembly** center where vehicles such as the space **shuttle** are put together. The **launching pad** is where the spacecraft are sent into space, and the **operations** center controls the launch.

The first American in space was Alan Shepard. He was the first person to go into space with the Mercury Program. His flight was only fifteen miunutes long. That was in 1961.

Less than a year later, John Glenn made three **orbits** around the earth. Later, in 1990, Glenn went into space again as a senior citizen.

Neil Armstrong was the first man to step on the moon. He went to the moon with two other astronauts, Mike Collins and Buzz Aldrin. He stepped on the moon on July 20, 1969.

People sometimes ask if space exploration is really worthwhile, especially after a **disaster**. The answer may be that it is human nature to explore the **universe**. Secondly, our **curiosity** about space and our exploration of space has resulted in the advancement of science and knowledge.

Exercises

C. Do you know these idioms and expressions? Work with a partner and put them in the sentences below.

As you can see	by then	Right on
put __ together	to say nothing of	all for it
got into	take _____ on	see eye to eye
glued to	First of all	check out

1. A: Do you want to see this program continued?
   B: Definitely! I'm _____ _____ ____. It's a great program.

2. America only _____ _____ the space race after the Russians launched Sputnik.

3. Would you be willing to _____ this new project ____? We need a strong leader for it, and we think you'll handle the responsibility well.

4. _____ ___ _____, let me thank you for inviting me to be on the program.

5. Let's go _____ _____ the rocket exhibit. I think it should be interesting.

6. _____ ___! I agree completely with you. You're absolutely right.

7. Who can forget it? We were all _____ ____ our TV sets, watching and waiting for more information.

8. ____ _____ _____ _____, we have done everything possible to make your visit enjoyable and interesting. You should have everything you need.

9. It was a difficult puzzle, but she _____ it _____ in less than one hour.

10. They firemen arrived at two o'clock, but ____ _____, it was too late. The building had burned down completely.

11. The cost of these vehicles is bad enough, ____ _____ _____ ____ the cost of operating them.

12. The two candidates will never _____ _____ ___ _____ on the need to spend money on space exploration.

Exercises

D. What do you remember? After you do the talk show, do this true or false review.

1. _____ Cape Canaveral was once called Cape Kennedy.

2. _____ The Kennedy Space Center was built in 1990.

3. _____ 300 spacecraft have been launched from Cape Canaveral.

4. _____ Mike Collins was the first American in space.

5. _____ Alan Shepard was in space for five hours.

6. _____ John Glenn orbited the earth three times.

7. _____ Neil Armstrong traveled alone to the moon.

8. _____ The NASA Launch Operations Center is in Houston.

9. _____ Armstrong stepped on the moon in 1990.

10. _____ It is possible to go and watch a launch.

Number right ____/10

E. Vocabulary Review. Finish these sentences.

1. _____ Canaveral is in Florida.

2. The Kennedy _____ Center is in Florida.

3. Over 3,000 _____ have been launched.

4. The Mercury _____ put a man in space.

5. John Glenn _____ the _____ three times.

6. Neil Armstrong climbed down the _____ and _____ on the moon.

The Exploration of Space   **65**

7. Glenn made another flight in 1990 as a _____ citizen.

8. The spacecrafts take off from a _____ pad.

Number right ____/10

A rocket launch at Cape Canaveral

F. These adjectives are used in the talk show. Can you use them?

____ famous	____ amazing	____ humble	____ far-fetched
____ huge	____ easy	____ excellent	____ impossible
____ large	____ tremendous	____ heady	____ careless

G. On a separate piece of paper, write your opinion: Space travel is/is not important because . . . .

H. Check out these websites on the internet. Take notes and report on your visit to your class.

www.ksc.nasa.gov   (Kennedy Space Center)

www.jsonline.com/news/nat/columbia   (Shuttle Columbia Disaster)

www.nasa.gov   (National Air and Space Administration)

Exercises

The Castillo de San Marcos
Spain in the New World

A. PREVIEW. Do you know these words? Look for them in the reading below.

____ colonization	____ voyage	____ possession	____ gunboat
____ struggle	____ fountain	____ war	____ invasion
____ power	____ empire	____ prison	____ heritage

B. Read this selection.

After Columbus discovered the New World in 1492, Spain was very active in the exploration and **colonization** of the Americas. In the 1500s and 1600s, several other European countries began to explore and colonize the New World. There was a **struggle** for land and **power**.

One early explorer was Juan Ponce de Leon. He first came to the New World on Columbus' second **voyage**. Later, he explored northern Florida and claimed it for Spain in 1513. There is a legend that he was also looking for the **fountain** of youth, a place where he could become young again. He also hoped to establish a colony, but he was killed in a fight with the Indians.

150 years later, the Spanish became nervous about their territory in Florida and their **empire** in the Americas because French and British **possessions** were not far away to the north. So the Spanish built a fort at Saint Augustine. It was called the Castillo de San Marcos. It is one of the oldest buildings in North America. It was completed in 1695.

The Spanish lost the fort to the British in 1763 as a result of the Seven Years' **War** which the British won. However, a few years later the American colonies and the British went to war. The Spanish governor of Louisiana, Bernardo de Galvez, helped the Americans by attacking the British along the Gulf Coast. Then, at the end of the American Revolutionary War, the Spanish again took over the fort.

Later, in 1821 Spain sold the fort to the Americans who named it Fort Marion, and used it mainly as a **prison**. For a short while, in the 1860s it was part of the Confederacy during the American Civil War. However, a northern **gunboat** easily captured it. After that, it was used once again as a prison for Native Americans who were resisting the **invasion** of their land. The fort was closed in 1900, turned into a national monument in 1924, and renamed the Castillo de San Marcos to honor its Spanish **heritage**.

All Around America   **67**

C. Do you know these idioms and expressions? Work with a partner and put them in the sentences below.

go back in time	too close for comfort	lock up
spend __ time	stopped in	let __ go
came back	come out on top	pack up
took control of	tied up	hit the road

1. I _____ ____ to see you yesterday, but you weren't there.

2. It's time to _____ ____ and load the car. Then we'll have breakfast. And at 9:00 we'll _____ _____ _____ and be on our way.

3. Only one team will _____ _____ ___ _____ and win the gold medal.

4. The Spanish _____ _____ ____ most of Latin America and much of the American West.

5. Let's ____ _____ ___ _____ to the discovery of the New World. Life on the continent was very different then.

6. The police questioned everyone, and after two hours they _____ them ____ home.

7. The speeding car almost hit us. It was ____ _____ ____ _____.

8. We couldn't get there on time. We were _____ ____ in traffic and couldn't move.

9. Someday, I'd like to _____ some _____ exploring Florida and the Gulf Coast.

10. He left suddenly, and he never _____ _____. We often wonder what happened to him.

11. I think that we should _____ ____ people like that and throw away the key.

Exercises

D. What do you remember? After you do the talk show, do this true or false review.

1. _____ The Castillo de San Marcos is the oldest building in the United States.

2. _____ Juan Ponce de Leon built the fort.

3. _____ Ponce de Leon died in Florida.

4. _____ The Seven Years' War is also known as the French and Indian War.

5. _____ Bernardo de Galvez was the governor of Louisiana.

6. _____ Galvez fought for the Americans during the American Revolution.

7. _____ At the end of the American Revolution, the British gave the fort to the Americans.

8. _____ The fort was used as a prison.

9. _____ The fort was once named Fort Marion.

10. _____ Five different flags have flown over the fort.

Number right _____/10

E. Vocabulary Review. Finish these sentences.

1. Several European countries wanted to establish _____ in the New World.

2. The Castillo de San Marcos is a star-shaped _____.

3. Ponce de Leon sailed with Columbus on one of his _____.

4. Ponce de Leon went looking for the _____ of youth.

5. To the north of Florida, the English and the French were not far away; they were too _____ for comfort.

6. At the end of the Seven Years' _____, the Spanish lost the fort.

7. Galvez attacked the British forts along the Gulf _____.

8. Florida joined the Confederate States during the _____ War.

9. A northern _____ captured the fort and Saint Augustine.

10. In 1886 many Apache Indians were _____ in the fort.

Number right _____ / 10

F. These adjectives are used in the talk show. Can you use them?

____ star-shaped	____ successful	____ grateful	____ fascinating
____ close	____ difficult	____ final	____ different
____ happy	____ victorious	____ complicated	

G. Write your opinion on a separate piece of paper: The United States *should/should not* become a bilingual country with English and Spanish as official languages.

H. Check out these websites on the internet. Take notes and report on your visit to your class.

www.nps.gov/casa   (Castillo de San Marcos)

www.oldcity.com   (City of Saint Augustine)

Fort Matanzas

www.nps.gov/foma   (Fort Matanzas)

www.hispanicamericanheroesseries.com/who.php   (Bernardo de Galvez)

Exercises

Washington, D.C.
A City of Memorials and Monuments

A. PREVIEW. Do you know these words? Look for them in the reading below.

____ capital	____ ambassadors	____ documents	____ marble
____ district	____ landlord	____ portrait	____ slab
____ square mile	____ tenant	____ tribute	____ sacrifice
____ oval office	____ First Lady		

B. Read this selection and underline any words you're not sure of. Write them below and find out what they mean.

The city of Washington, D. C. is the nation's **capital**. D. C. means the **District** of Columbia. The district covers 67 **square miles**, and it does not belong to any state. It's a favorite tourist place, and there is much to see.

The White House is where the president works. His office is called the **oval office**. He often meets important visitors such as other presidents and **ambassadors** in his office. The President and his family also live in the White House, but the American people own the White House. They are the **landlord** and the President is a **tenant.**

When the British invaded Washington in 1814, they burned the White House. **The First Lady** was Dolley Madison, and she managed to save many valuable **documents** before escaping. She also saved a historic **portrait** of George Washington.

The Washington Monument was constructed after Washington died. It is a **tribute** to America's first president. It is possible to climb to the top of the monument. The view from the top is wonderful.

The Lincoln Memorial is a massive **marble** building. Inside is a statue of Lincoln, looking down at you. It is very impressive.

The Vietnam Memorial was created by a young woman, Maya Lin. It is a huge **slab** of black granite that forms a wall. The names of all the American men and women who died in Vietnam are carved into the wall. It is a moving tribute to their **sacrifice**.

Exercises

C. Do you know these idioms and expressions? Work with a partner and put them in the sentences below.

wind up	pure luck	wouldn't hear of it
be willing to	burned down	lit up
look around	was away	What about
set up	at once	scratched the surface

1. Please do this ____ _____. We've got to have it now!

2. The city was all _____ ____ for the festival — lights everywhere.

3. I _____ _____ when it happened, and didn't hear about it until I got home.

4. I hope you have time to _____ _____ while you're visting the city. There's a lot to see.

5. A: Where shall we go?
   B: _____ _____ the Jefferson Memorial? Have you seen it?

6. Would you ____ _____ ____ help me for a little while?

7. And so this is where we _____ ____ our tour of the city. I hope you enjoyed it.

8. Winning the lottery is just _____ _____, whereas winning at Blackjack requires some skill.

9. While they were away, their house almost _____ _____, but the fire department got there right away and saved the building.

10. This tour of the city has only _____ _____ _____. It would take years to learn about everything that has happened here.

11. I offered her money for her help, but she _____ _____ ____ ____. She said she was happy to help out.

12. So, let's _____ ____ a meeting with all the department heads — Tuesday at nine.

Exercises

D. What do you remember? After you do the talk show, do this true or false review.

1. _____ The city of Washington is in the state of Virginia.

2. _____ The Oval Office is in the White House.

3. _____ The president's office is across the street from the White House.

4. _____ The fourth president of the U.S. was Abraham Lincoln.

5. _____ In 1814, the White House was burned by the British.

6. _____ Dolley Madison saved many valuable documents.

7. _____ There are stairs inside the Washington Monument.

8. _____ There is a statue of Lincoln at the Lincoln Memorial.

9. _____ The Vietnam Memorial is a granite wall.

10. _____ Maya Lin was the architect of the Vietnam Memorial.

Number right _____/10

***Washington Memorial,
Washington, D.C.***

E. Vocabulary Review. Finish these sentences.

1. D.C. means the _____ of Columbia.

2. The district occupies 67 _____ miles.

3. The president's office is _____ in shape.

Exercises

4. Dolley Madison was the First _____ in 1814.

5. The British tried to _____ down the White House.

6. Dolley saved a _____ of George Washington.

7. The Washington _____ is 555 feet high.

8. The Lincoln Memorial is a _____ building.

9. The Vietnam Memorial is a black _____ wall.

10. The names of those who died in the Vietnam war are _____ into the wall.

Number right _____/10

F. These adjectives are used in the talk show. Can you use them?

____ federal	____ near	____ impressive	____ real
____ sightseeing	____ proud	____ massive	____ simple
____ true	____ brave	____ gorgeous	____ moving

G. On a separate piece of paper, write about the capital of your native country, or the capital of your state. Where is it located? How long has it been the capital. What is special about it?

H. Check out these websites on the internet. Take notes and report on your visit to your class.

www.washington.org (Washington tourism)

www.whitehouse.gov (The White House)

www.thedistrict.com (The District of Columbia)

Answers to the Exercises

1. Statue of Liberty *page 3*

C. Idioms and Expressions
1. on the line 2. take freedom for granted 3. By the way ... one and the same 4. tune in 5. In the first place 6. stands for 7. knock the statue down 8. coming up 9. near and dear 10. in person 11. Absolutely 12. ran out of

D. True or False
1F 2T 3F 4F 5F 6T 7T 8T 9F 10F

E. Vocabulary Review
1. beacon 2. framework 3. pedestal 4. torch 5. crown 6. stands for 7. sculptor 8. huge 9. harbor 10. construct/build/ make/complete

2. Boston *page 7*

C. Idioms and Expressions
1. sick and tired 2. on the way 3. fans the flames 4. out of the question 5. hot on their trail 6. filled in 7. better half 8. got away 9. all over again 10. stand by ... jump in 11. stood their ground ... underway 12. ran away

D. True or False
1F 2T 3F 4T 5F 6F 7F 8T 9T 10T

E. Vocabulary Review
1. wife 2. redcoats 3. defended 4. taxes 5. march/go 6. lantern/light 7. fortify/occupy 8. attacked 9. retreated 10. casualties

3. Lowell *page 11*

C. Idioms and Expressions
1. named after 2. a great deal of 3. On the one hand 4. put out 5. keep up ... shut down 6. take advantage of 7. pick up ... wrap it up 8. in my mind 9. grew up 10. dropped out 11. laid off

D. True or False
1F 2T 3T 4F 5F 6T 7F 8T 9T 10F

E. Vocabulary Review
1. birthplace/showplace 2. textiles/cloth 3. flows/flowed 4. turbines 5. showplace 6. immigrants ... pour/come 7. boardinghouses 8. Canada 9. success 10. ethnic/cultural

4. Gettysburg *page 15*

C. Idioms and Expressions
1. break away 2. after ... after ... turned the tide 3. this very spot 4. turning point 5. In a nutshell 6. takes place 7. go on 8. a matter of time 9. hold ... off 10. broke the back 11. take a look

D. True or False
1T 2F 3F 4T 5F 6T 7T 8T 9F 10F

E. Vocabulary Review
1. Civil 2. independent 3. seceded 4. president 5. opposed 6. Southern 7. battles 8. Northern/Union 9. Gettysburg Address 10. slaves/slavery

5. Chicago *page 19*

C. Idioms and Expressions
1. in ruins 2. in harmony with 3. dies hard 4. fielded the question 5. How about 6. kick off 7. What do you say 8. hot air 9. by the time 10. kicked up 11. As a matter of fact 12. blows away

D. True or False
1F 2T 3T 4T 5F 6T 7F 8T 9F 10T

E. Vocabulary Review
1. skyscraper 2. lantern 3. architects 4. environment/surroundings 5. framework 6. feet 7. Windy 8. homeless 9. elevator 10. ashes

6. St.Louis *page 23*

C. Idioms and Expressions
1. take on 2. pass ... up 3. got together 4. get in touch with 5. find out 6. couldn't say enough 7. took off 8. bring ... down 9. head up 10. would you care to 11. another matter 12. In fact

D. True or False
1F 2T 3F 4F 5T 6F 7F 8F 9T 10T

E. Vocabulary Review
1. gateway 2. continent 3. Purchase/Territory 4. expedition . . Discovery 5. interpreter 6. canoe 7. pioneeers 8. architect 9. flood

7. Mt. Rushmore *page 27*

C. Idioms and Expressions
1. out of work 2. sorry to say 3. ringing off the hook 4. touch and go 5. Among other things 6. can hardly wait 7. had in mind 8. get a kick out of 9. passed away 10. call on 11. got caught up in 12. As time goes by

D. True or False
1T 2T 3F 4T 5T 6F 7F 8T 9T 10T

E. Vocabulary Review
1. sculptor 2. mountain 3. feet 4. granite 5. birth 6. preservation 7. depression 8. dangerous 9. stonecutters/workers 10. Pyramid

8. The Oregon Trail *page 31*

C. Idioms and Expressions
1. as well as 2. word spread 3. in short 4. move in 5. on our doorstep 6. went off 7. time was up 8. on your mind 9. pointed out 10. so to speak 11. thumbnail sketch 12. boiled down

D. True or False
1F 2T 3F 4T 5F 6F 7T 8T 9F 10F

E. Vocabulary Review
1. wagons 2. miles per hour 3. River 4. Divide 5. Pass 6. missionary 7. mission 8. Valley 9. cholera 10. diseases

9. Alaska *page 35*

C. Idioms and Expressions
1. How come 2. turned into 3. striking it rich 4. not to mention 5. no picnic 6. on top of all that 7. get rid of 8. right away 9. make fun of 10. pipe dream 11. took ... for every cent 12. bottom fell out of

D. True or False
1T 2F 3T 4F 5F 6T 7F 8T 9F 10T

E. Vocabulary Review
1. explorer 2. fur 3. trading 4. State 5. acre 6. discovered . . . prospectors 7. Trail 8. tourism 9. Inuit

10. Hawaii *page 39*

C. Idioms and Expressions
1. wiped out 2. took over 3. one at a time 4. go back 5. settle down 6. trade places 7. the scoop 8. Better late than never 9. As you know 10. make sure 11. a foothold 12. take ... up on

D. True or False
1F 2T 3T 4F 5T 6T 7T 8F 9T 10F

E. Vocabulary Review
1. paradise 2. Polynesians 3. Kingdom 4. Missionaries 5. banned 6. Aloha 7. constitution 8. monarchy 9. Republic 10. active

11. The Golden Gate Bridge *page 43*

C. Idioms and Expressions
1. changed my mind 2. stick around 3. take it all in 4. as the story goes 5. to name a few 6. came up with 7. get it 8. looks as if 9. bring ... up 10. come about 11. cleared ... up 12. came upon

D. True or False
1F 2T 3F 4T 5T 6F 7F 8T 9F 10T

E. Vocabulary Review
1. blend 2. Strait 3. suspension 4. towers . . . cables 5. pedestrians 6. schedule . . . budget 7. Bay 8. mile

12. Grand Canyon *page 47*

C. Idioms and Expressions
1. take ... chances 2. did ... in 3. and all 4. put it into words 5. call ... up 6. put ... on the map 7. on edge 8. walk in the park 9. getting ahead of myself 10. speaking of 11. Now you're talking 12. better off

D. True or False
1T 2F 3T 4F 5F 6T 7T 8T 9T 10F

E. Vocabulary Review
1. wide ... deep 2. reservation 3. rapids 4. professor 5. gold ... minerals 6. conservation 7. rafting 8. national

13. Mesa Verde *page 51*

C. Idioms and Expressions
1. moved away 2. if I may 3. talk ... over 4. dug up 5. get up 6. In other words 7. simply put 8. looked up to 9. get down 10. pulled ... up 11. had no choice 12. as far as we know

D. True or False
1T 2T 3F 4F 5F 6T 7F 8F 9T 10T

E. Vocabulary Review
1. Mesa 2. tribe 3. descendants 4. ladders 5. dwellings 6. drought 7. Archeologists 8. Basket . . baskets 9. Hopi 10. elders

14. The Alamo *page 55*

C. Idioms and Expressions
1. go after 2. showed up 3. iron hand 4. give up 5. pinned down 6. get out 7. beefed up 8. tells it like it is 9. not about to 10. push me around 11. time heals all wounds 12. hold out

D. True or False
1F 2T 3F 4T 5T 6F 7F 8F 9F 10F

E. Vocabulary Review
1. mission 2. Christianity 3. independent/free 4. dictator 5. rebels 6. reinforcements 7. ammunition 8. Remember 9. commander 10. country

15. New Orleans *page 59*

C. Idioms and Expressions
1. hooked on 2. put on 3. all over 4. That is to say 5. way back 6. get started 7. let loose 8. can't beat 9. Of all the 10. had a ball 11. get going 12. call it quits

D. True or False
1T 2F 3T 4F 5F 6F 7T 8T 9F 10T

E. Vocabulary Review
1. ethnic 2. unique 3. Mardi Gras . . party 4. Creole 5. gourmet 6. jazz 7. trumpet 8. concert 9. French

16. The Kennedy Space Center *page 63*

C. Idioms and Expressions
1. all for it 2. got into 3. take ... on 4. First of all 5. check out 6. Right on 7. glued to 8. As you can see 9. put ... together 10. by then 11. to say nothing of 12. see eye to eye

D. True or False
1T 2F 3F 4F 5F 6T 7F 8F 9F 10T

E. Vocabulary Review
1. Cape 2. Space 3. spacecrafts 4. Program 5. orbited the earth 6. ladder and stepped 7. senior 8. launching

17. The Castillo de San Marcos *page 67*

C. Idioms and Expressions
1. stopped in 2. pack up . . . hit the road 3. come out on top 4. took control of 5. go back in time 6. let ... go 7. too close for comfort 8. tied up 9. spend ... time 10. came back 11. lock up

D. True or False
1F 2F 3T 4T 5T 6T 7F 8T 9T 10T

E. Vocabulary Review
1. colonies 2. fort 3. voyages 4. fountain 5. close 6. War 7. Coast 8. Civil 9. gunboat 10. imprisoned

18. Washington, D.C. *page 71*

C. Idioms and Expressions
1. at once 2. lit up 3. was away 4. look around 5. What about 6. be willing to 7. wind up 8. pure luck 9. burned down 10. scratched the surface 11. wouldn't hear of it 12. set up

D. True or False
1F 2T 3F 4F 5T 6T 7T 8T 9T 10T

E. Vocabulary Review
1. District 2. square 3. oval 4. Lady 5. burn 6. portrait 7. Monument 8. marble 9. granite 10. carved

Grizzly bears catching salmon in Alaska.